TIME OUT
THE DAVE BRUBECK QUARTET

DAVE BRUBECK

PAUL DESMOND

JOE MORELLO

EUGENE WRIGHT

According to the Chinese calendar, 1959 was the Year of the Pig. But music fans will be excused if they prefer to recognize it as the *Year of the Jazz Masterpiece.* Was there ever a more action-packed 12-month period in the history of the art form? Will there ever be another burst of creativity in jazz to match it? By my reckoning, we are more likely to live to see the Year of the Pigs Who Sprout Wings.

What happened in 1959? John Coltrane released his seminal *Giant Steps* LP, his first recording built entirely on his original compositions. Thelonious Monk presented a historic concert at Town Hall and recorded a stunning solo piano album in San Francisco. Ornette Coleman shook things up with *Tomorrow is the Question, The Change of the Century* and *The Shape of Jazz to Come.* Duke Ellington provided a Grammy®-winning soundtrack to *Anatomy of a Murder.* Charles Mingus released *Mingus Ah Um, Mingus Dynasty* and *Blues & Roots.* And you know it must be a competitive scene when Sonny Rollins needs to stop performing and practice some more... which he did in grand style, building his legend by walking the Williamsburg Bridge with tenor in hand, back in '59.

Of course, we shouldn't forget a gentleman named Miles Davis, who began work on *Sketches of Spain* with Gil Evans in 1959 and recorded his biggest selling album of all time, *Kind of Blue.*

Yet, in the midst of that star-studded year, Dave Brubeck had the grandest success of them all with his mind-expanding album *Time Out.* Even *Kind of Blue* didn't achieve the type of sales Brubeck's recording racked up in those first years after release. "Take Five," the surprise

Macero and Brubeck at Newport, 1963

radio hit from *Time Out,* would become the first million-selling jazz instrumental single on the *Billboard* Hot 100. Five years earlier, Brubeck had become the first modern jazz musician to appear on the cover of *Time* magazine, but that unprecedented achievement now just seemed a warm-up for this new burst of fame and recognition.

The music from *Time Out* crossed over in a way that no previous modern jazz recording had even approached. Talking about "Take Five," superstar Billy Joel would later acknowledge that the song "was as important to me as *Sgt. Pepper's* was to rock-and-roll aficionados in the 1960s." In the aftermath of Brubeck's success, the "Take Five rhythm"—a 5/4 bar divided into a waltzy 3/4 followed by two-beat kicker with an emphasis on beat four—was popping up in places far beyond the confines of the jazz world: on the theme to the TV series (and later movie) *Mission Impossible,* in rock band Jethro Tull's hit single "Living in the Past," in Nick Drake's "River Man." In recent years, I have encountered hip-hop, reggae, salsa and other "beyond jazz" versions of "Take Five." Arrangements have been written for marching band, flute choir, string orchestra, and even handbells. Jazz critic Doug Ramsey recalls finding a wooden music box in a little shop off of Betlémská in Prague which, when opened, played the first eight bars of Paul Desmond's melody.

But *Time Out* was much more than just "Take Five." "Blue Rondo à la Turk," a tour de force in 9/8 and 4/4, which opened the album, was one of the great jazz performances of the era, and even today there

TIME OUT

Desmond seemed to have stepped out of an alternative universe in which bebop had never existed. Desmond's tone was warm and sweet at a time when cutting and acerbic were the norms, and his musical personality—a paradoxical mixture of the cerebral and the tender—was a concoction of his own invention. No one sounded like Paul Desmond then. No one sounds like Paul Desmond today.

Both Brubeck and Desmond were Westerners, with all of the spirited independence that term conveyed during their formative years. Dave Brubeck had been born in 1920 in Concord, California, and spent much of his youth on a ranch in Ione so large it spanned three counties. Paul Desmond was also a native Californian, but never needed to wear a cowboy hat during his childhood in San Francisco, where he had been born in 1924.

Their oddly congruent yet contrasting mature musical styles seemed to reflect these early differences. Brubeck's music, for all its experimental zeal, was never airy-fairy, but retained an earthiness and a vigor that kept things grounded; along the way, he tossed out as many surprising moves as a bull just out of the shoot at the rodeo. Desmond, for his part, was the urban sophisticate, and his playing summed up images of stylish parties in penthouse apartments. He once famously said he wanted his alto sound to "sound like a dry

This new single, "Blue Rondo a la Turk" and "Take Five", is part of a new album by the Dave Brubeck Quartet titled "Time Out", which is soon to be released.

These two originals, one by Brubeck and the other by Paul Desmond, his alto saxophone player, contain a new direction in Jazz. New time signatures, 9/8 and 5/4 time, are used in this single. In the complete album you'll find many other innovating time signatures.

Most Jazz as we know it today is in 2/4, 4/4, and sometimes 3/4, but here we have a new approach.

The Brubeck Quartet has given the Jazz improviser new fertile ground on which to improvise. This is exciting and new.

martini"—a quip he may have regretted given the flippant image it portrayed—yet the comparison was apt. While other saxophonists captured the ambiance of roadhouses and juke joints, Paul Desmond's playing seemed to evoke a slightly louche black tie event.

But it would take a dynamo from the East Coast to serve as the catalyst who made *Time Out* possible, and drummer Joe Morello filled this role to perfection. This virtuoso percussionist, born in Springfield, Massachusetts in 1928, was a dramatic performer whose flamboyant style was out of character with the previous drummers in Brubeck's various ensembles. His arrival in the quartet completely changed the sound of the group—so much so that Desmond threatened to quit unless Morello were fired. The two eventually reconciled and became close friends, but only Brubeck's mediation and daring conception of his future musical direction held the quartet together during this period of (in the words of *New Yorker* writer Robert Rice) "bloody war" in the band.

Bassist Eugene Wright, born in Chicago in 1923, may have had less solo space than the other members of the classic Dave Brubeck Quartet, but his contribution was also essential to the success of *Time Out.* Without his rock solid time and big sound it is hard to imagine the ensemble achieving such admirable cohesion while navigating through the odd time signatures and compositional twists and turns of Brubeck's visionary project.

During this same period, the role of the bass was changing in modern jazz. The younger generation was playing the instrument as though it were a big guitar, straying from the ground beat and generally adopting a lighter, less dominating tone. But Eugene Wright was old school, a throwback to the Kansas City style of pre-war jazz, when the bassist's beat was as dependable as that grandfather's clock in the family homestead that hasn't missed a tick or a tock since the Calvin Coolidge administration. With Wright (known affectionately as "The Senator") on bass, the beat in the Quartet was so certain, the rest of the band could loosen up—they knew that the man with the pulse was taking care of business.

Even with this illustrious group of accompanists, Brubeck's success with *Time Out* was a surprise, especially considering how overworked the pianist had been in the period leading up to the session. Brubeck had been composing, recording and performing at a prodigious pace— he had recorded a dozen projects in the previous three years, including a number of now classic albums such as *Jazz Impressions of Eurasia, Gone With the Wind, Dave Digs Disney* and *Jazz Impressions of the USA.* To fulfill his obligations to the Fantasy label, he had also appeared

on *Reunion* and *Solo Piano*. Brubeck also made a number of live recordings during this period including *Jazz Goes to Junior College, Newport 58* and *The Dave Brubeck Quartet In Europe.* As if this wasn't enough, Brubeck agreed to serve as musical ambassador as part of an innovative State Department program—so now, in addition to all his other commitments, he found himself bringing his distinctive brand of pianism to Poland, Turkey, Pakistan, Ceylon, Iran, Iraq and Afghanistan. With all due respect to James Brown, it would have been difficult to find a harder working man in show business during these years than Dave Brubeck.

And Brubeck never just went through the motions on the road. As the previously unissued tracks from Newport, included with this set, make clear, the Quartet thrived on the energy and unpredictability of working in front of an audience. Listen, for example,

"Kathy's Waltz" is dedicated to Dave's daughter Cathy
(misspelled due to a typographic error by Columbia Records).

to the hot and hard version of "Take Five" from 1964, especially to the interaction between piano and drums during Brubeck's solo, and you will understand that this band never did anything by rote, even with songs they played at every concert. Fans who caught the Dave Brubeck Quartet during those long road trips of the 1950s and 1960s were never quite sure what they might hear on stage. But if it was any consolation, they could at least rest assured that the musicians themselves hardly had a better idea of what was going to happen next.

Any other artist would have been burnt out by the constant demands of this unsustainable schedule. And in India, Brubeck came down with dysentery, returning home sick, feverish and malnourished. Yet he also brought back new musical ideas from these trips. "I was on my way to a radio station to be interviewed in Turkey," Dave recalled when I conducted an oral history with him in 2008. "I was walking

through the streets; there were street musicians playing in 9/8 [he sings a 9/8 rhythmic pattern—a combination of three groups of two beats followed by one group of three]. Like that . . . I thought to myself, boy, when I get home, I'm going to write a tune . . . I'll put harmony to it, and my own melody. That's how I started 'Blue Rondo à la Turk.'" Wherever Brubeck traveled, he sought out inspiration for his compositions (check out the version of "Koto Song" from *Newport '64,* for another example of his pioneering interest in what we now call "world music"), but this new focus on unusual meters would prove to be the most fruitful experiment of his long career.

Yet here, as throughout the history of the Quartet, the other band members would add their own unique contributions to Brubeck's strange new project. Before *Time Out,* Joe Morello had been toying with 5/4 rhythms, slipping them into his solo work to add a different flavor to the music. And Paul Desmond, the least avant-garde member

of the band—perhaps the least avant-garde jazz star of his generation—provided the pièce de résistance with his composition "Take Five."

The song almost never came about. Desmond toyed with a couple of ideas: one was a poignant melody over a lilting minor-ish vamp and the other a major-key romp that quickly modulated through a sequence of two chords per bar. Brubeck had the insight to blend these together into a single song, and the contrast between the two themes no doubt contributed to the song's appeal. Desmond himself had few illusions about his work. "I was ready to trade in the entire rights to 'Take Five' for a used Ronson electric razor," he once remarked with his characteristically self-effacing wit. A far better measure of Desmond and his memorable song can be found in his last will and testament which, upon his death in 1977, bequeathed the royalties from "Take Five" (and his other compositions) to the American Red Cross, which receives a six-figure annual income from this gift.

Columbia Records sell sheet for the 1961 release Time Further Out (note the photo credits are reversed).
Appealing to record store buyers, the back page continues with the punch line "...Take Five and Act!"

SINCE "TAKE FIVE":

· Since "Take Five" was released several months ago, it has sold close to A QUARTER OF A MILLION COPIES.

· "Take Five" has spurred the "Time Out" album into the NUMBER 2 position on the Billboard album chart. At this writing the album is heading for A QUARTER OF A MILLION COPIES!

· DEMAND HAS INCREASED FOR THE ENTIRE BRUBECK ALBUM CATALOG. ALL OF DAVE'S ALBUMS HAVE EXPERIENCED STRONG NEW SALES ACTION AS A RESULT OF THIS NEW BRUBECK EXPOSURE.

· SINCE "TAKE FIVE," DAVE BRUBECK'S AUDIENCE HAS VASTLY EXPANDED. Even the "squarest" of the square are beginning to see the light!

· Unquestionably THE most heavily programmed jazz group in the country. The door is now wide open for Top 40, pop, R & B and jazz programming with every type of DJ swinging with Brubeck as never before.

· Since "Take Five," Brubeck has become a stronger juke box attraction than ever before - in every type of location.

· NEW SINGLE - "IT'S A RAGGY WALTZ"/"UNSQUARE DANCE" and NEW ALBUM - "TIME FURTHER OUT" KICKING OFF TO FABULOUS EXPOSURE AND SALES!

CONCLUSION:

THIS IS A PHENOMENON IN THE RECORD INDUSTRY. NEW AVENUES OF EXPOSURE FOR BRUBECK ARE WIDE OPEN; PUBLIC ACCEPTANCE AND AUDIENCE DEMAND IS GREATER THAN EVER BEFORE. BEST SELLING JAZZ ARTIST IS BECOMING OUT-AND-OUT HIT ARTIST. ONLY COLUMBIA HAS BRUBECK; HIS RECORDS CANNOT BE COVERED. YOU ARE RIDING THE TAIL OF A COMET. THIS IS THE START OF SOMETHING BIG. HERE'S WHAT YOU MUST DO:

Brubeck Quartet and
New York Philharmonic

Brubeck and his A&R
man - Producer Teo Macero

Blue Rondo a la Turk by the Dave Brubeck Quartet brings to jazz a unique
combination of elements from three different musical cultures. Dave added
his own theme and harmonic pattern to an ancient Turkish Rhythm. These
raw materials were shaped into an early European Classical Form -- The Rondo
which merges into the Blues. In this EP version we hear one chorus of the Blues
development.

1000 words

to be -- v d known

TIME OUT
THE DAVE BRUBECK QUARTET

50th ANNIVERSARY

Produced by
Alfred Music Publishing Co., Inc.
P.O. Box 10003
Van Nuys, CA 91410-0003
alfred.com

Printed in USA.

ISBN-10: 0-7390-6233-6
ISBN-13: 978-0-7390-6233-3

Album artwork courtesy of **Sony Music Entertainment**

BLUE RONDO Á LA TURK

Music by Dave Brubeck

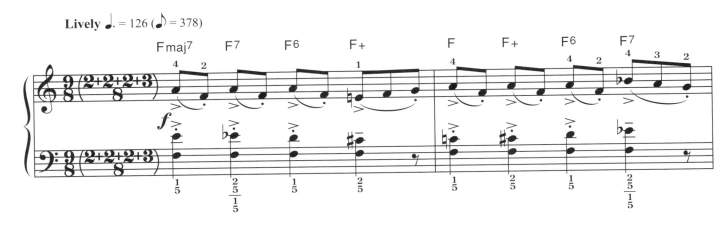

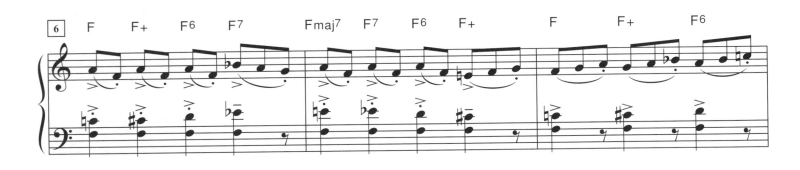

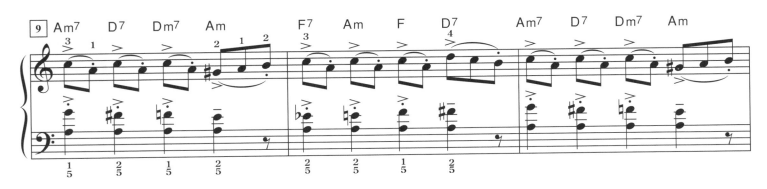

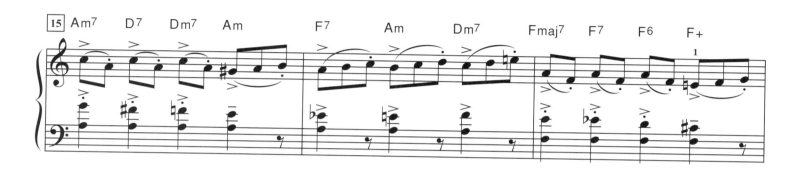

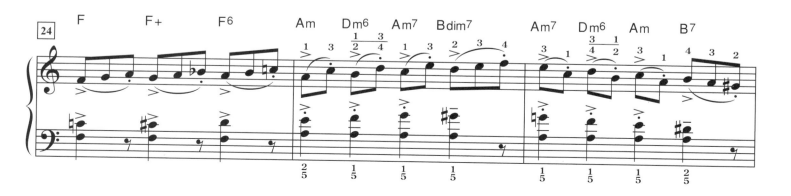

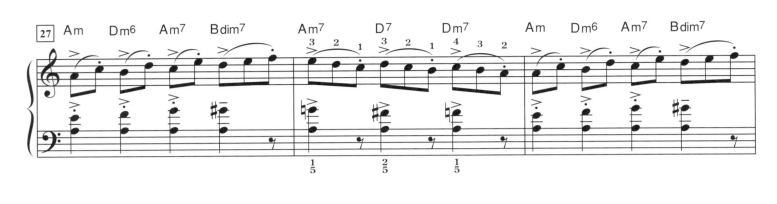

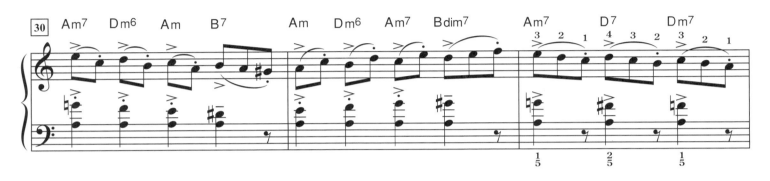

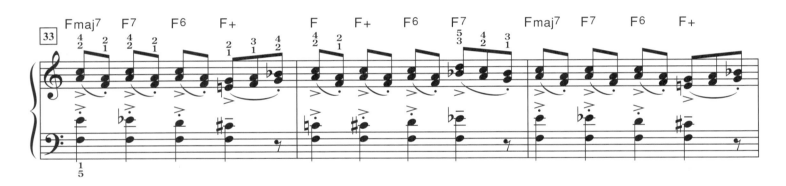

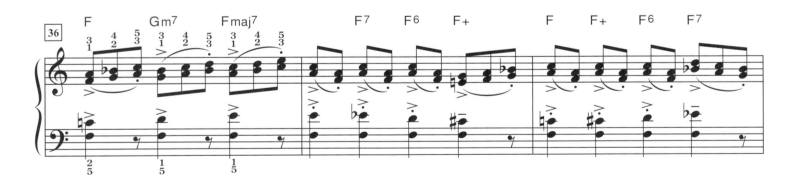

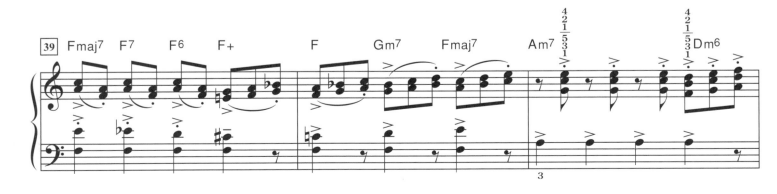

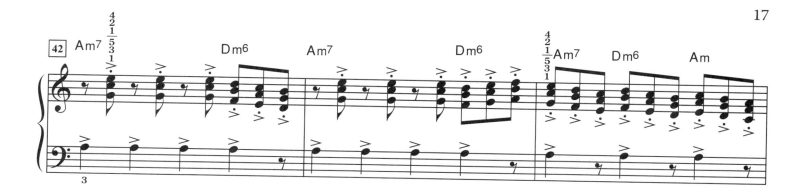

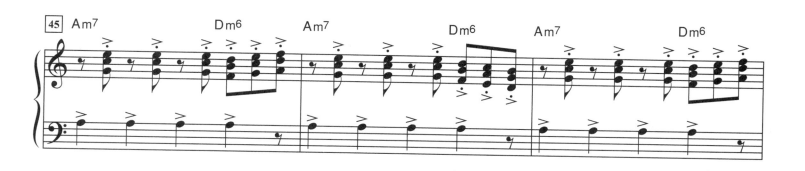

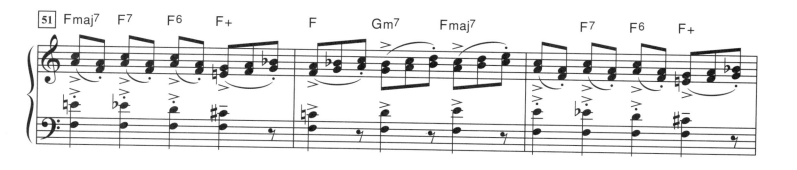

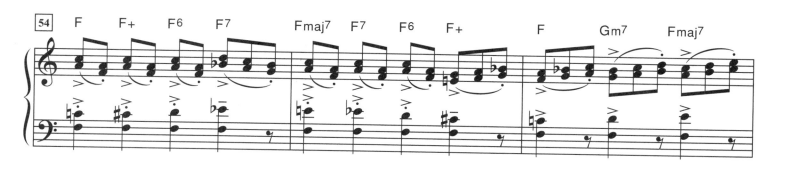

18

STRANGE MEADOW LARK

Words by Iola Brubeck
Music by Dave Brubeck

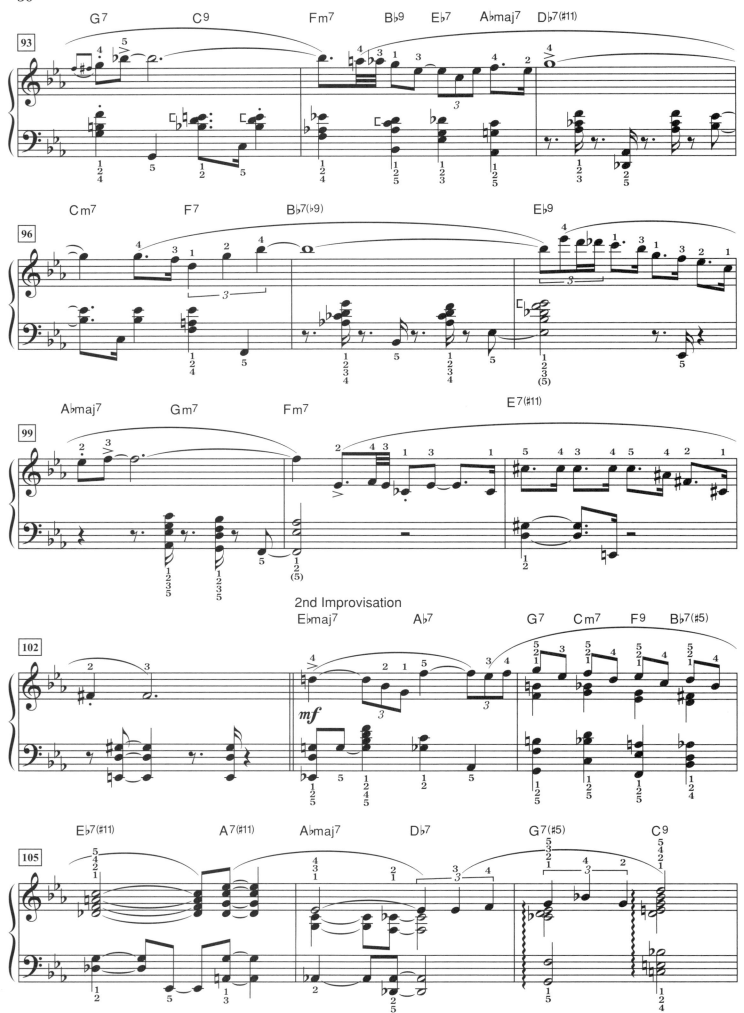

32

TAKE FIVE

Music by Paul Desmond

35

37

38

THREE TO GET READY

Music by Dave Brubeck

2nd Improvisation

KATHY'S WALTZ

Music by Dave Brubeck

2nd Improvisation

EVERYBODY'S JUMPIN'

Music by Dave Brubeck

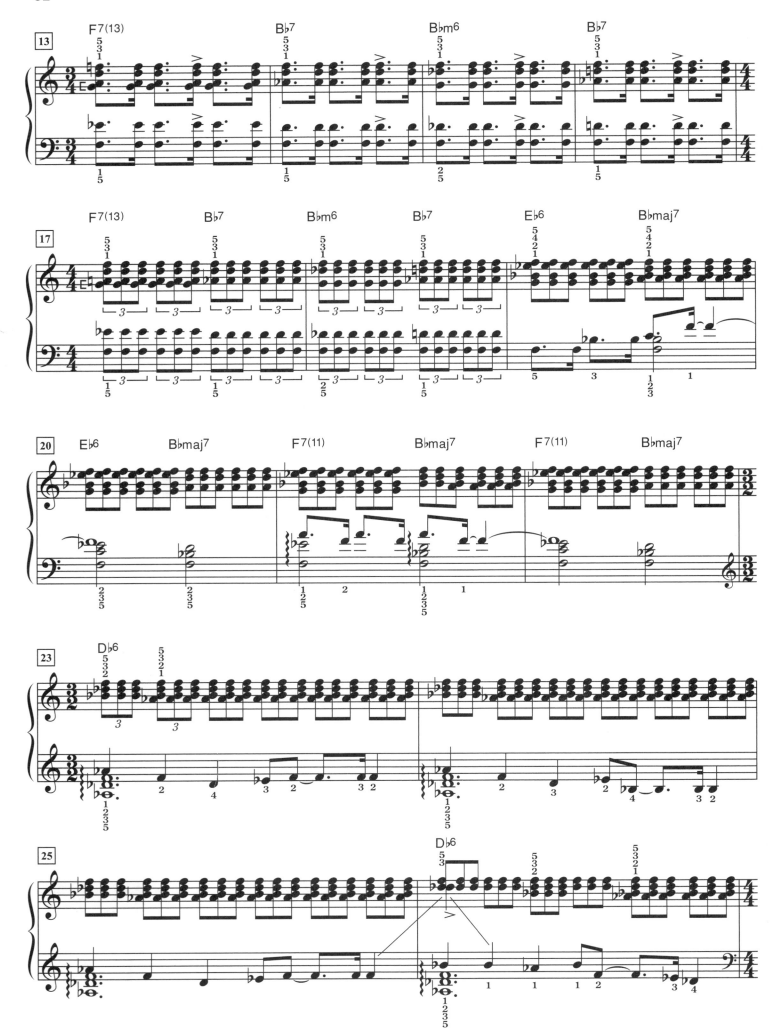

54

56

* Either the C or the E♭ may be omitted, if necessary.

PICK UP STICKS

Music by Dave Brubeck

The upper note of the bass pattern should be very soft.
The chord of B♭7 is used throughout.

2nd Improvisation

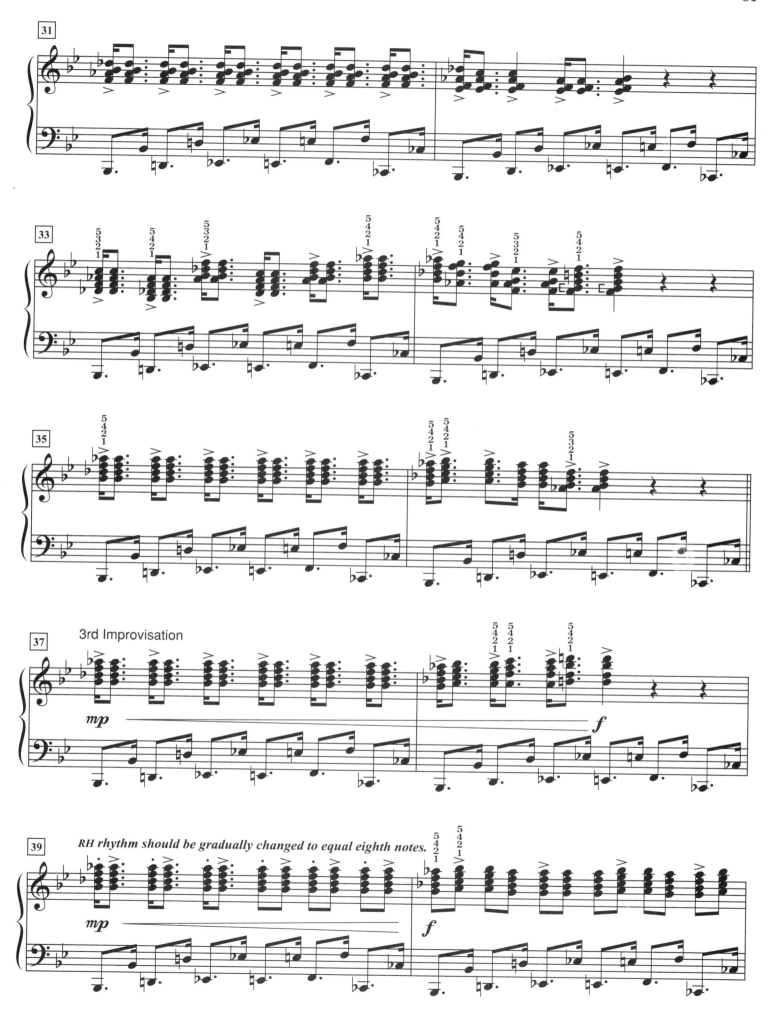

3rd Improvisation

RH rhythm should be gradually changed to equal eighth notes.